# Modern World Religions:
# Judaism

CW00428176

Anne Geldart

Heinemann Educational Publishers
Halley Court, Jordan Hill, Oxford, OX2 8EJ
a division of Reed Educational and Professional
Publishing Ltd

OXFORD  MELBOURNE  AUCKLAND
JOHANNESBURG  BLANTYRE  GABORONE
IBADAN  PORTSMOUTH (NH)  USA  CHICAGO

Heinemann is a registered trademark of Reed
Educational and Professional Publishing Ltd

First published in 2002

06 05 04 03 02
10 9 8 7 6 5 4 3 2 1

**British Library Cataloguing in Publication Data**
A catalogue record for this book is available from the
British Library

ISBN 0 435 33642 8

Picture research by Jennifer Johnson
Typeset by Artistix, Thame, Oxon
Printed and bound in Spain by Edelvive

**Acknowledgements**
The publishers would like to thank the London Beth Din,
Kashrut Division, for permission to use the kosher
certificate, p. 19.

The publishers would like to thank the following for
permission to use photographs: Andes Press Agency/
Carlos Reyes-Manzo, pp. 14,  16 (bottom right), 23 (top),
24 (top), 43; BFI Stills, p. 2 (left); The Bridgeman Art Library/
Galleria degli Uffizi, Florence, p. 5;  The Bridgeman Art
Library/Magyar Nemzeti Galeria, Budapest, p. 58; The
Bridgeman Art Library/The Mass Gallery, London, p. 12;
The Bridgeman Art Library/Museum of the City of New
York, p. 49; Camera Press/Titti Fabi, p. 3 (right); Camera
Press/Amram Galmi/Imapress, p .13; Camera Press/Lee
Lynx, p. 6;  Camera Press/Greg Marinovich, p. 28; Camera
Press/Richard Stonehouse, pp. 3 (left), 8; Camera
Press/Kevin Unger, p. 48; Corbis,  p. 56; Mary Evans
Picture Library, p. 55; Impact/John Evans, p. 52; Alex
Keene, p. 17; Performing Arts Library/Mark Douet, p. 2
(right); Zev Radovan, pp. 10, 15 (left), 16 (bottom left and
top right), 20, 21, 23 (bottom), 24 (bottom), 37, 38, 42;
Science Photo Library/Gordan Garradd, p. 50; Science
Photo Library/Royal Observatory, Edinburgh, p. 59;
Science Photo Library/TEX Image, p. 53, Science Photo
Library/Hattie Young, p. 40; Juliette Soester, pp. 15
(right), 18, 25, 33, 34, 45, 46.

The publishers have made every effort to contact
copyright holders. However, if any material has been
incorrectly acknowledged, the publishers would be
pleased to correct this at the earliest opportunity.

**Websites**
Links to appropriate websites are given throughout the
book. Although these were up-to-date at the time of
writing, it is essential for teachers to preview these sites
before using them with pupils. This will ensure that the
web address (URL) is still accurate and the content is
suitable for your needs.

We suggest that you bookmark useful sites and consider
enabling pupils to access them through the school
intranet. We are bringing this to your attention as we are
aware of legitimate sites being appropriated illegally by
people wanting to distribute unsuitable and offensive
material. We strongly advise you to purchase suitable
screening software so that pupils are protected from
unsuitable sites and their material.

If you do find that the links given no longer work, or the
content is unsuitable, please let us know. Details of
changes will be posted on our website.

**The Bible**
Jews call the Bible Tenakh. It is mainly written in Hebrew,
but some parts are in Aramaic, a language similar to
Hebrew. The Tenakh has three parts: Torah (the Five
Books of Moses), Nevi'im (the books of the Prophets) and
Ketuvim (holy writings). In this book, whenever we say
'the Bible' it is the Tenakh that we refer to. For English-
speaking pupils, the quotations are taken from English
translations and can be found in the school Bible.

**Tel: 01865 888058   www.heinemann.co.uk**

# Contents

# Introduction to Judaism

In this section you will:

- learn why it is important to study religions so that we can know about what people believe and how this affects the way they live
- consider how studying religion helps us to think about questions such as 'Why are we here?' and 'Does God exist?'

## What is Judaism?

**Judaism** is the name of the religion that Jewish people follow. It began with Abraham in about 2000 BCE. Judaism started in the land now called Israel, but from 70 CE, most Jews have lived in other countries.

Christians and Muslims share many of the beliefs of the Jews. They use stories and teachings of the **Tenakh** (the Hebrew Bible).

The Tenakh is like a library of books, arranged in three sections. These are the **Torah** (first five books), the **Nevi'im** (prophets) and **Ketuvim** (holy writings). You will learn more about the Tenakh later in this book.

Judaism is a **monotheistic** religion. That is, Jews believe in only one God. This God is the creator of all things, and judges all people.

Many Jews believe God chose them to be his people. He made a **covenant** (promise) with them. They must follow the laws that God revealed to Moses. The Ten Commandments are the most important of these laws, and Christians and Muslims, as well as Jews, think they are important today.

*Joseph on the West End Stage*

*Moses' story in* The Prince of Egypt

*Vanessa Feltz, a famous Jewish television presenter*

Jews also believe that Israel (the country) is important to their history, as well as in the present day.

## Stories of importance

Many films and musicals are based on stories from the Tenakh. These stories are also shown in pictures in art galleries.

In today's world, there are many famous Jews. Jonas Salk developed the polio vaccine. Michael Marks (of Marks & Spencer) and entertainers Barbara Streisand and Woody Allen are also Jewish.

The writers and thinkers Sigmund Freud and Karl Marx were from Jewish families.

The book *The Diary of Anne Frank* is about the suffering of the Jews in World War II.

*Woody Allen, a famous Jewish film-maker*

## Learning about religion

❶ 'There is no need to learn about the Jewish faith.' What would you say to someone to show that it does matter?

❷ 'What parts of the Jewish religion do Christians and Muslims share?

❸ 'Write down the names of some plays, films and musicals that are based on Jewish stories.

## Learning from religion

❶ Why do you think stories are important to people?

❷ Write a talk about the achievements of one of the Jewish people mentioned in this section.

# Abraham

In this section you will:
- understand how most Jews regard Abraham as one of the founders of the Jewish faith
- learn how Abraham obeyed God's calling.

## An easy life?

It would be nice to have an easy life, with money, servants and not having to work – being able to relax.

There was a man called Abram, who was very rich. He lived about 4000 years ago in the city of Haran in modern-day Iraq. He was married to Sarai. Abram believed God told him to leave his home and go and search for a new land. He was quite old, and had to start a new life with his wife, and their nephew, Lot.

*Living the easy life*

## Abram becomes Abraham

You can read about this in Genesis, the first book of the **Tenakh**.

In those days, a name was important because it said something about the person's character. Abram meant 'exalted father'. When Abram proved himself to be obedient to God, he was re-named Abraham, which means 'Father of nations'. His wife's name, Sarai, was also changed to Sarah, which means 'princess'.

These name changes marked the beginning of a special relationship between God and the descendants of Abraham. Jews believe this was the **covenant**, an agreement in which God says 'I will be your God and you shall be my people'.

The sign of the covenant was **circumcision**. This is where the foreskin of a boy's or man's penis is removed by a surgical operation. Jews continue this tradition today.

## Destruction of Sodom and Gomorrah

Abraham, Sarah and Lot, their nephew, travelled towards the new land that God had promised them. Lot decided to leave and go to live in the city of Sodom and a neighbouring city of Gomorrah.

The ancient story tells that the people in these cities were very wicked and God decided to destroy them. Abraham prayed to God to ask if some good people could be saved. Lot was saved. His wife was told not to look back at the city. She did look back – and was turned to a pillar of salt.

## Sacrifice

Abraham and Sarah wondered when they would have the son that God had promised them. Then, when they were quite old, Sarah became pregnant. They named their son Isaac.

When Isaac was twelve years old, Abraham believed that God wanted him to offer his son as a sacrifice. He took him to a high mountain, and was just about to offer him as a sacrifice when he heard a voice telling him to stop. The voice told him to kill a ram that God had provided instead.

This was a sign that God does not want human sacrifice. He wants people to be obedient to Him.

*Abraham, about to sacrifice Isaac*

### Learning about religion

❶ Read the story in Genesis 22 about Abraham and Isaac. Why do you think this story may be important to Jews today?

❷ Many Jews today think Abraham was a good example for them to follow. Why do you think this is?

### Learning from religion

❶ God promised things to Abraham. With a partner, discuss whether it is always right to keep your promises. Can there be times when it is not right to do so?

❷ The story of Lot's wife is a way of saying that we should not look back on the past. Should we try to forget the past or learn from it?

❸ Abraham was obedient to God. With a partner, try to write a list of 'orders' you should obey, and another of those you might not.

# Moses

In this section you will:

● think about what makes a good leader

● learn about the importance of Moses as a leader who obeyed God

● think about what it means to be 'called by God'.

## What makes a leader?

A leader is someone who other people choose to follow. Leaders may have a strong personality and a clear idea of where they want to lead people. Modern politicians are examples of leaders.

## Moses the leader

Several hundred years after Abraham, the Jews had become slaves of the Egyptians. Moses was a Jew, but he was adopted by the Egyptian royal family when he was a baby. One day, he saw a Jewish slave being beaten by a slave master.

*David Ben-Gurion, a modern Moses*

This made him angry and he killed the slave master. He ran away, and eventually met and married Zipporah, the daughter of a man who owned many thousands of sheep. Moses became a shepherd.

One day he thought he saw a bush that was burning but was not being burnt up. He believed that God was telling him to return to Egypt and put things right for the Jews.

At first Moses did not want to go. He felt he was not the right man for the job. But then he became convinced that God had called him to set the Jewish people free, and that he must obey.

Some people believe that Moses saw a bush that really was on fire and heard the voice of God. Others believe Moses had a 'vision' – a mind-picture – of the bush on fire.

## The Passover

Moses went to Pharaoh, the king of Egypt, and told him that God said, 'Let my people go'. Pharaoh refused. Then ten plagues happened. A plague is a disease or terrible event. Moses said that God sent the plagues. This helped the Jews to believe that God had chosen Moses to be their leader. Moses told them that God was on their side and was trying to help them.

Still Pharaoh refused to let the Jews go. Then in a final plague, the Angel of Death visited each house and killed the oldest child. The Angel of Death passed over the homes of the Jews. They had smeared lamb's blood on their door-posts to show

Many Jews today see Moses as an important role model. He is seen as a good leader, and one who was obedient to God. He is also the one who taught the Jews about the Law and about justice.

*The ten plagues sent to Egypt*

they were Jews. This is now called **Pesach**, which means 'Passover'. Pharaoh finally let the Jews go and they escaped from Egypt. This escape is called the **Exodus**.

## The lawgiver

Moses led the Jewish people to Mount Sinai. There, tradition says, he met God face to face and received God's teachings, the **Torah**, which includes the Ten Commandments.

Finally, after forty years, Moses led the people to the border of the land that he said God had promised them. However, he died before they entered the Promised Land.

### Learning about religion

❶ From what you have read in this section, explain why Moses is so important to Jewish people.

❷ Read Exodus 3: 1–12. Draw a series of pictures to show the story of the Burning Bush.

### Learning from religion

❶ a What makes a good leader? Make a list of qualities that you think a good leader needs.

  b Choose three leaders you know about and describe their jobs. What leadership qualities do they have?

❷ We all have to live by rules. Working with a partner, choose two different situations where there are rules. Why is it a good idea to have rules do you think?

❸ Are there any rules that you have to obey that you think are unfair? If so, how would you go about changing these rules?

# *Elijah*

In this section you will:
- think about how to deal with things that are wrong
- learn about Elijah, an important **prophet** and leader of the Jewish people.

## Good anger

Sometimes it is right to get angry. In 1985, Bob Geldof, a rock musician, was very angry because people were starving in Africa. He thought people were not doing enough to help. He organized a charity concert called Live Aid. This raised over £40 million.

*Bob Geldof's anger helped millions through Live Aid*

## Elijah gets angry

Jews believe that all through history, God sent prophets to tell people His message. They tell people what God says is wrong with the world, and call them to be more obedient to God. In this way, they can help to bring about a better world. One of the most important of these prophets is Elijah. You can read about him in your Bible, in 1 Kings: 17–19.

He lived in about the ninth century BCE when King Ahab and Queen Jezebel ruled Israel. Elijah thought the King and Queen were leading the people to worship false gods.

## Showdown at Mount Carmel

Queen Jezebel came from Sidon, where the people worshipped Baal. She wanted the Jews to worship Baal, too, and had over 450 prophets to encourage them to do so.

Elijah became angry and believed God wanted him to take on these prophets of a false god.

He challenged them to a contest on Mount Carmel, the 450 prophets of Baal on one side, and Elijah alone on the other. They each prayed to their god to set fire to their sacrifices. It was Elijah's prayer that succeeded, and his sacrifice that was consumed by fire. This was a sign that God was the true and only God.

*Earthquake, wind and fire*

said he was rude about the king and about God. He could be put to death for this.

When Elijah heard about it, he confronted Ahab. Ahab asked for God's forgiveness.

## The end of the story

Tradition says Elijah never died but was taken directly to heaven in a chariot. Many Jews today believe that Elijah will return when the **Messiah** (God's representative) is coming to the earth. At the annual celebration of **Pesach**, an empty chair is set at the table. This is called Elijah's chair.

## A still, small voice

After this, Queen Jezebel wanted to kill Elijah, so he went into hiding. He was scared, depressed and alone. He hid in a cave, and prayed for God to appear to him.

There was an earthquake, but God did not appear. Then there was a fire, but God still did not appear. Then Elijah heard a still, small voice and this was God, speaking to him. This shows that God can be known in small events, as well as in exciting, spectacular events.

## Naboth's Vineyard

If anyone inherited land in Israel, they were not allowed to sell it to the King. This was the law. King Ahab noticed his neighbour, Naboth, had a vineyard next to the palace. He wanted to buy it, but Naboth refused.

Ahab was upset, so his wife, Queen Jezebel hired two men to lie about Naboth. They

### Learning about religion

❶ Which of the following words describe Elijah? Give reasons for your answer. *Weak, strong, caring, thoughtful.*

❷ Why do many Jews think Elijah is important today?

❸ Write the story of Naboth's vineyard as a play or poem.

### Learning from religion

❶ Give an example of when it is right to get angry.

❷ What can people do when those in power are not doing the right thing?

❸ Use the Internet or your school library to find out about the work of the Jewish National Fund and Jewish care organization such as Norwood Child Care.

# Beliefs 1 – God and the covenant

In this section you will:
- learn why belief in one God is important to Jews
- understand why the **covenant** is important.

## Promises, promises

We often feel hurt or disappointed when people don't keep their promises to us. We depend on promises. For example, marriage involves promises between two people to love and care for and be faithful to each other.

Jews believe that God has promised to care for them and has chosen them to be His people. In return they must be faithful and obedient to Him. This is called the covenant.

Jews believe God made the first covenant with Noah after the flood (Genesis 9) and gave the rainbow as a sign that He would never destroy the whole world again.

The second covenant was with Abraham, when God promised him many descendants (Genesis 12 and 17). This was renewed with Moses when God gave him the Ten Commandments and other teachings that the people had to follow.

> 'I am the Lord your God, who brought you out of the land of Egypt, out of the house of slavery. You shall have no other gods besides me.'
>
> Exodus 20: 2–3

When Jewish families have their sons circumcised (see pages 40–1), or their children become **Bar Mitzvah** or **Bat Mitzvah** (see pages 42–3), they are confirming the covenant.

*Marriage involves making promises*

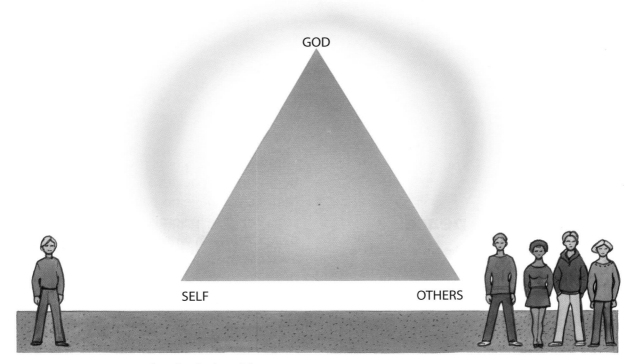

GOD

SELF

OTHERS

*Martin Buber's triangle of relationships*

## Monotheism

'Hear, O Israel! The Lord is our God, the Lord is one. You shall love the Lord your God with all your heart, and with all your soul and with all your might.'

Deuteronomy 6: 4

This quotation is called the **Shema**. 'Shema' is Hebrew for 'hear'. The Shema is written on a small scroll of parchment called a **mezuzah** (see pages 14–15) and put in a small case that is fixed to the doorposts of many Jewish homes.

The idea of having one God is called **monotheism**. Jews were one of the first groups to believe in one God who creates everything, and keeps everything going. He is Judge and King of the Universe. Jew believe they must not worship **idols**.

The Jewish thinker, Martin Buber, wrote a book called *I and Thou*. He said people needed a relationship with God and this would help them to have proper relationships with each other.

### Learning about religion

❶ What are the two main ideas about the covenant between God and the Jews?

❷ In what ways is marriage like the covenant between God and the Jews?

### Learning from religion

❶ Is it always right to keep your promises? Give reasons.

❷ How might believing in God affect the way people behave?

# Beliefs 2 – shalom

In this section you will:
- learn about the Jewish idea of **shalom**
- reflect on (think about) what 'peace' means to you.

## Give me some peace!

There does not seem to be much peace in our world. People fall out

- at school
- at home with their relatives
- anywhere they get together.

We read about wars in the newspapers and wonder if there has ever been any peace in the world.

*The dove of peace*

## So, what is peace?

Jews often use the word 'shalom' in place of 'hello' or 'goodbye'. It is the Hebrew word for 'peace'.

Some Jewish teachers say that peace begins inside you. If you are in a bad temper, you have no peace inside you, so you cannot help someone else to find peace. A Jewish writer, Louis Jacobs, says, 'Peace is the fruit of inner strength.'

It is important to have peace within the family. Parents and children must all try to live in a peaceful way.

Jewish people believe that sometimes it is right for people to fight in wars. However, they long for a time when wars will cease.

There are many different groups within **Judaism**. They have differing thoughts about their religion. Many believe an age of peace will come when God sends his Anointed One, Mashiah (**Messiah**).

The **prophet** Isaiah describes the age of peace like this:

The wolf shall live with the lamb.
The leopard with the kid.
The calf and the young lion will be together
and a little child shall lead them.
The cow and the bear shall graze,
their young shall lie down together;
the lion shall eat straw like the ox.
The nursing child shall play
over the hole of the asp,
and the weaned child shall put its hand on the adder's den.

They will not hurt or destroy on all my holy mountain:
for the earth will be full of the knowledge of the Lord
as the waters cover the sea.

Isaiah 11: 6 (contemporary English version)

Peace is about bringing opposite sides together, so that they understand each other. This is what Isaiah was saying in his word-picture of nature coming together.

Let the sun rise to light the morning,
Even the purest prayer will not awaken
Bitter tears will not revive, will not bring back
Those whose candle was put out and buried in the dust.
Don't say a day will come, seize that day
for it is not a dream
And in all the squares
Shout out a song for peace!

## The Song of Peace

Israel's Prime Minister, Yitzak Rabin, was assassinated in 1995 while he was trying to bring peace to the country of Israel. He was carrying in his jacket pocket a poem written by two Jewish men called *The Song of Peace*.

*Yitzak Rabin, Prime Minister of Israel, was assassinated for his beliefs*

### Learning about religion

❶ Write out a modern version of Isaiah's vision of peace.

❷ Most Jews are not pacifists. Use a dictionary to find out what this word means.

### Learning from religion

❶ What could you do to make life more peaceful at home, in school and in the world? Working in groups, 'brainstorm' your ideas and make a spider diagram.

❷ Are there times when it is right to fight? Give reasons for your answer, showing that you have though about it from more than one point of view.

# Signs and symbols 1

## What is a symbol?

A symbol is something that stands for something or someone else. A sign is a picture or gesture that is used instead of words.

Symbols are often used in religion. They may convey ideas that are too difficult to put into words.

## Magen David Adom

No one knows for sure when the Star of David (**Magen David Adom**) became a symbol in the Jewish faith. It may have been an ancient Hindu symbol.

*The Magen David Adom*

An image of this star was found in a **synagogue** in Capernaum from the first century CE.

When Adolf Hitler came to power in Germany in the 1930s, he ordered Jews to wear the Star of David. This made it easier for the Nazis to identify them. By the end of World War II, the Nazis had murdered six million Jews.

After the War, when the country of Israel was set up, the new country included the Star of David in its national flag.

## The menorah

In many religions, light is an important symbol for good. The **menorah** was part of the official 'furniture' of the ancient temple. Today most **synagogues** have a menorah. It is a six-branched candleholder.

A special, eight-branched candleholder called a **hanukiah** is used at the celebration of **Hanukkah**, in the winter.

## The mezuzah

'These commandments which I have given you this day are to be remembered and taken to heart; repeat them to your children…Bind them as a sign upon your hand and wear them as a pendant on your forehead; write them on the door posts of your houses and on your gates.'

Deuteronomy 6: 6–9
(Contemporary English Version)

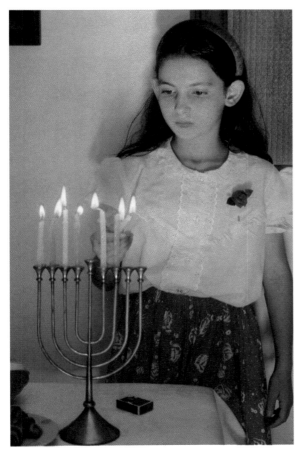

*This girl is lighting the hanukiah*

*A mezuzah is often found on every door of a Jewish home*

If you visit a Jewish home today, you may see small containers like the one above.

This is a **mezuzah** case and is fixed to the door frame of every room in the house except the bathroom. It contains a small scroll on which is written the **Shema**.

Even actions or gestures can be symbols. For example, folding the hands and bowing the head when praying are symbols of humility. The action of lighting a candle is symbolic of the first action of God in creation when He said, 'Let there be light'.

## Learning about religion

❶ Write a poem called 'Magen David'.

❷ Why do you think light is used as a symbol in many religions?

❸ Why do many Jewish families attach a mezuzah case to the door posts in their homes?

## Learning from religion

❶ When the Nazis entered Denmark, the King ordered all his people to wear a Star of David. Why do you think he did this?

❷ Do you think it is important to remember bad things that happened in the past? Give reasons for your answers.

15

# *Signs and symbols 2*

*The tefillin*

## What matters to you most?

If your house caught fire, what would you save first? It might be a toy or a computer or a photograph that means a lot to you. Some things will be more important to you than others.

## Tallit

Many Jewish people wear a **tallit** when they pray. This is a prayer robe or shawl. A full-size tallit is about 2 metres by 1.5 metres.

## Tefillin

**Tefillin** are small leather boxes which contain tiny scrolls. The **Shema** prayer is written on the scrolls. They wear them on their head and their arm as a sign that they are true to God.

*The tallit*

*The kippah*

*The mikveh is used for ritual bathing*

Men visit the mikveh before **Yom Kippur**, an important Jewish festival. Men and women visit the mikveh before the marriage ceremony. Women visit the mikveh after their monthly period has ended or after childbirth.

The idea behind this is that the person must be clean inside as well as outside. By dipping themselves under the water of the mikveh, Jewish people believe they have become purified and so fit to talk to God in prayer.

## Kippah

A **kippah** is a cap that some Jews wear all day, while others wear a kippah only for prayer. The kippah may be plain, or decorated with symbols such as the **Magen David Adom**. It is a sign of humility to God.

## The mikveh

The **mikveh** is a special pool where people can immerse themselves to be purified. This is not about physical cleanliness. A Jew would have to be clean outside even before going into the mikveh.

## Learning about religion

❶ Why do you think wearing a kippah can be a sign of humility to God?

❷ How is a mikveh important to many Jews?

## Learning from religion

❶ What do you own that you really value? Is 'expensive' the same as 'valuable'?

❷ What does it mean to humble? Can anyone know if they really are humble?

❸ What do you think is the difference between being clean and being pure?

# Kosher food

In this section you will:
- learn about the importance of **kosher** food to Jewish people
- reflect on how what people eat and how they prepare it shows what kind of people they are.

## You are what you eat

Food is important to everyone. A vegetarian does not eat meat products. A vegan will avoid anything that comes from animals, such as milk or cheese. What people eat or refuse to eat shows what they believe.

## Kosher food

The word kosher means clean, pure and fit to eat. Many Jews try to follow the laws about what they can and cannot eat from the **Torah**.

The book of Leviticus, the third book of the Torah, gives rules about food that is fit to eat. When the book of Leviticus was written, the ancestors of the Jews lived in the deserts. The food rules were for their good health. Now Jews obey them as an act of obedience to God.

As a general rule, animals that have cloven (divided) hooves and chew the cud are fit to eat. This means cows, sheep and goats are kosher. Pigs, rabbits and horses are not kosher.

Fish are kosher if they have fins and scales, like trout and cod. Shell-fish and prawns are not kosher.

Birds such as chicken, duck and turkey are allowed, but birds of prey are not kosher.

Eggs and milk are kosher if they come from kosher birds and animals.

*There are many different types of kosher food*

Vegetables and fruit are neutral. They are allowed, as long as they are clean and are carefully checked for bugs and 'creepy-crawlies'.

Strict Jews also try to obey the rule that says they must not eat meat and milk foods at the same meal. In an **Orthodox** (very strict) Jewish home, there are often two sinks, sets of crockery and cutlery for milk and meat foods.

For strict Jews, it is important that kosher food is properly labelled. Some supermarkets have special kosher sections. Kosher food usually has a special label on it to show that a **rabbi** has approved it.

Some years ago there was a rumour that Coca-Cola was made in a non-kosher way. The company was so concerned that they invited a leading rabbi to visit one of the plants where Coca-Cola is made. He approved it – Coca-Cola was declared to be kosher.

Sometimes, Jewish people set up their own shops and have their own butchers.

In London's East End, a group of Jews set up a Kosher Luncheon Club. They specialized in fish dishes. It became popular with lots of people who lived in the area, not just Jews.

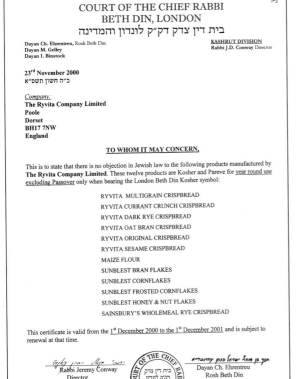

*A kosher food certificate*

## Learning about religion

❶ Why do you think some Jews believe that it is important to follow the kosher food laws?

❷ Design a leaflet or poster to show what foods are kosher.

❸ Say which of the following foods are kosher, giving reasons for your answer: potato, smoky bacon, fresh orange juice, rabbit pie.

## Learning from religion

❶ Many people are careful about what they eat. Do you think that what you eat matters? Why do you think this is?

❷ Canteens in schools and offices must provide for people with different eating habits. How could they ensure they provide the best for their customers?

# Worship at home 1 – Shabbat

In this section you will:
- think about the need for rest and time to think
- learn about the importance of the day of **Shabbat** to Jews.

## Holy days and holidays

Everyone needs to take some time off from work. Originally, days of rest and relaxation were linked with holy days. Now any time off is called a holiday.

Weekends are an important time to rest for most people. For Jews, weekends are special.

Jews measure a day from sunset to sunset. From sunset on Friday to sunset on Saturday is a day of rest for Jews and it is called by the Hebrew word Shabbat (Sabbath). Some Jews measure Shabbat from a set time on Friday (say 6pm) to the same time on Saturday.

## Why is there Shabbat?

'On the seventh day, having finished all his work, God blessed the day and made it holy, because it was the day when he finished all his work of creation.'

Genesis 2: 2–3

'Remember to keep the Sabbath day holy. You have six days to labour and do all your work, but the seventh day is the Sabbath of the Lord your God; that day you must not do any work, …for the Lord made the heavens and the earth in six days, the sea and all that is in them, and on the seventh day he rested. Therefore the Lord blessed the Sabbath day and called it holy.'

Exodus 20: 8–9

These verses from the **Torah** explain why Jews observe Shabbat. It is a weekly day of rest to remember and be thankful to God for His work of creation.

# Shabbat today

Before Shabbat begins, the family must clean the house and get it ready. All the shopping must be done before Friday evening. The table will be set with the 'best' tablecloth, cutlery and plates.

Some Jewish men and women go to the **synagogue** on Friday evening, while others will go on Saturday morning.

Just before Shabbat, the mother of the family lights two candles and says a special prayer to welcome in this day of rest. She says a blessing for her family and the candles are a symbol of joy and peace.

The father blesses his chidren and says the **kiddush** (blessing) over a cup of wine. The family sits down to a meal together.

On the table are two plaited loaves called **challot** (singular **challah**). These remind Jews of the double-helping of **manna** (special bread) that God provided in the desert when they had escaped from Egypt. This was so they would not have to work on Shabbat.

No work must be done on Shabbat, and Jews try to avoid anything that encourages work. For some Jews, this means that even turning on a light must be avoided, although some have automatic timers for ovens and lights.

**Havdalah** is a ceremony that marks the end of Shabbat. The word means 'separation'. There is a spice box that is passed round as a symbol of hope for good things to come during the week ahead, and a plaited candle to remind Jews that God's first act in creation was to make light. There are more blessings:

- over a last cup of wine

- over the spices to show that the spiritual part of the week has gone and the 'ordinary' day is about to begin

- over the candle-flame to show that Jews may once again light a fire, and finally, a blessing to thank God for providing a holy day of rest.

*A spice box*

## Learning about religion

❶ What reasons does the Bible give for keeping Shabbat a holy day?

❷ Write about three symbolic acts that take place at Shabbat.

## Learning from religion

❶ Do you think people need a weekly day of rest? Give reasons for your answer.

❷ The Jewish greeting at Shabbat is 'Shabbat shalom' – 'a peaceful Sabbath'. How could you bring peace to the coming week?

# Worship at home 2 – prayer

In this section you will:
- learn about the importance of worship at home to Jewish people
- think about the way that doing things together brings a family closer together.

## Worship begins at home

Jews believe that it is good for a family to pray together. It helps them to think about each other's needs.

At many festivals, including **Shabbat**, Jews may worship at home and at the **synagogue**.

In **Orthodox** synagogues women do not pray aloud. But many women lead the prayers at home.

## Why pray?

The family is very important to Jews. They believe that the **covenant** between God and the Jews means they should try to get closer to God. They can do this through prayer.

They may also pray if they need to ask for something for themselves or someone in need. However, Jews believe they must only pray for good reasons. They must not pray for evil or selfish reasons.

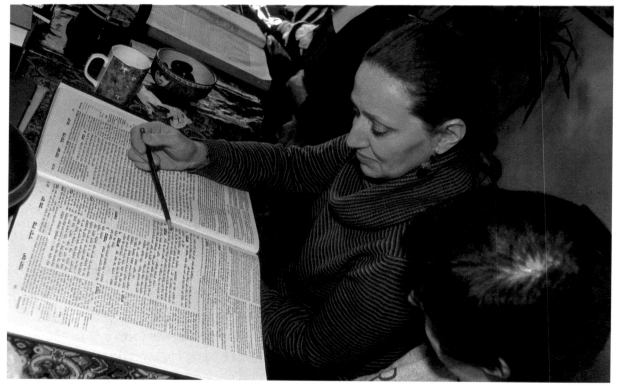

*Reading the Siddur*

Jews also pray to thank God for the good things He has done for them. They worship God because they believe He created the world, and it was He who rescued the people of Israel from slavery in Egypt.

## Types of prayer

Most Jews use a prayer book called a **Siddur**. This contains prayers they can use at home or the synagogue. These are printed in Hebrew, but some have English translations alongside.

Prayers begin with the **Shema** (see page 16). This is followed by the **amidah** – eighteen benedictions, or blessings. Each one ends with:

'Blessed art Thou, O Lord our God, King of the Universe.'

Many of the prayers come from the Bible, such as this one:

'Holy, holy, holy, is the Lord of Hosts, The whole earth is full of your glory.'

Most of the time Jews pray standing, but may bow as they refer to God as King. At certain high holy days, such as **Yom Kippur** (see pages 32–3) Orthodox Jews may kneel as a sign of humility before God. For prayer, Jewish men and some women wear the prayer robe or **tallit**, and a **kippah** and **tefillin** (see page 16).

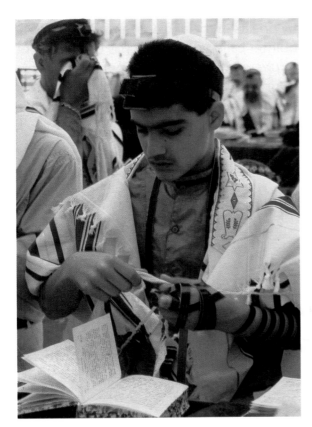

*Ready for prayer*

### Learning about religion

❶ Write down three reasons why Jews pray. Is one reason more important than others?

❷ How might prayer help a Jewish family to come closer together?

❸ Working in groups, find out more about the objects used in prayer. Make a collage of pictures of these objects. Label it.

### Learning from religion

❶ 'Prayer is a waste of time.' How might a Jewish person answer this? What do you think?

❷ 'What matters most in prayer is your intention, not your actions while you are praying.' Discuss.

# Worship in the synagogue

In this section you will:
- learn why the **synagogue** is important to Jewish people
- learn what happens there.

## Places that matter

We all have special places, places that matter to us. It may be the place we were born, or where we go on holiday.

For Jewish people, the places where they meet to worship God have always been special. For about a thousand years, until the first century CE, they worshipped in a temple in Jerusalem and in local places of worship. When the temple was destroyed, they worshipped in synagogues.

## The synagogue

The word synagogue means a place of meeting. The Hebrew for this is **Bet ha Knesset**. The synagogue may also be called the House of Study or the House of Prayer.

## What do you see inside a synagogue?

Every synagogue has a cupboard called **Aron Hakodesh** (the Ark). This is where the scrolls of the **Torah** and other holy writings are kept. The scrolls may be 'dressed' in a mantle of expensive cloth.

*The Torah scrolls are taken from the Ark*

The shield represents the breastplate worn by priests in the ancient temple. There is a pointer called a **yad** which is used to point to the words on the scrolls when reading during services. The bells look like crowns and remind worshippers that the Torah is the teaching of the great King – God.

Sometimes families pay for new scrolls in memory of an important event in their lives.

*Yad pointers come in a variety of styles*

*Inside a synagogue*

Above Aron Hakodesh is **Ner Tamid**, the perpetual light. This is a sign of God's **covenant**. Also above the Ark are two tablets, which represent the Ten Commandments given to Moses.

In the centre of the synagogue is the **bimah**, a raised platform. On this is a reading desk, where the scrolls rest while readings of the **sidra** (portions of scripture) take place.

An important person at synagogue services is the **rabbi**, who is leader of the synagogue. His main role is to teach and explain the Torah. Another is the **cantor**, who leads the singing in the services. There are also **wardens**, who help people to find their seats.

There are differences between **Orthodox** and **Reform** synagogues, which we will look at in the next section.

Important events take place at the synagogue, such as **Bar Mitzvah**, **Bat Mitzvah** and weddings. Sometimes families pay an annual sum for the upkeep of the synagogue and to pay the salary of the rabbi and other staff at the synagogue.

## Learning about religion

❶ Why do Jews go to the synagogue?

❷ Describe or draw three items that are in a synagogue. Why are they important?

❸ Do you think families should pay to belong to a synagogue?

## Learning from religion

❶ 'You can be religious without other people about.' How might a Jew answer this? That would you say?

❷ 'You don't have to go to a synagogue to be a Jew.' How might a Jewish person respond to this statement?

# Orthodox and Reform synagogues

In this section you will:
- learn about **Orthodox** and **Reform synagogues**
- think about differences that exist within a religion.

## Tradition or change?

Not so long ago a computer would fill a whole room. Now we can fit one into a watch. Television and the Internet help us to see what is happening all over the world. Women have more rights than they did in years gone by.

Is all change good? Is it sometimes better to let things stay as they are?

Religious people have to face this problem, too. They have to decide whether to keep their religion as it was when it first began, or bring it up-to-date.

## Jewish groups

Secular Jews are not religious, but feel they belong to their Jewish roots. **Ashkenazim** are Jews whose ancestors came from Eastern Europe. **Sephardim** are Jews who can trace their families back to Spain and North Africa.

Two of the largest Jewish groups are Orthodox Jews and Reform Jews.

Orthodox Jews believe they should keep to the old ways. They believe it is right to observe the traditions and festivals as set out in the **Torah**. They believe these teachings are still relevant today.

They look forward to the coming of the **Messiah**, who will bring a time of peace.

Reform Jews believe you can adapt the old teachings to present-day situations. For example, they believe that the **kosher** food laws were right when Jews lived in the desert. They think it is not necessary to keep these laws now because we have modern methods of storing and cooking food. They believe that every Jew should work to bring peace into the world. It is not right to wait for a Messiah figure to bring a golden age.

In Orthodox synagogues, men and women sit separately. In Reform synagogues, men, women and children all sit together.

Orthodox synagogues always have a male rabbi, while in the Reform synagogue there may be a male or female **rabbi**.

Orthodox families start their **Shabbat** at sunset on Friday, which varies throughout the year. Reform families tend to start at 6pm on Fridays.

*Inside an Orthodox synagogue*

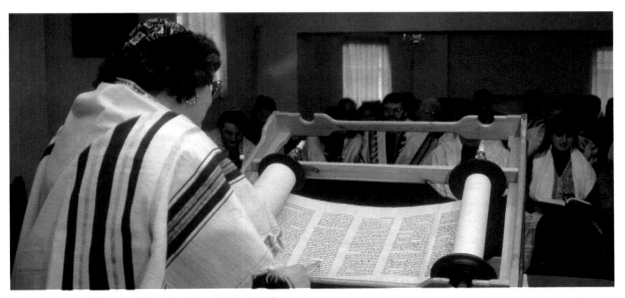

*A woman rabbi reading the Torah in a Reform synagogue*

In an Orthodox synagogue in Britain, the Shabbat service is in Hebrew, except for the prayers for the royal family and the State of Israel. In Reform synagogues, more of the service is in English.

In Orthodox synagogues there are only males in the choir and no musical instruments are used. Reform synagogues may have a mixed choir and an organ to accompany the singing.

The **minyan** – a minimum of ten people for public worship to take place – in an Orthodox synagogue must be men. In Reform synagogues the minyan may contain women.

All synagogues have prayer services throughout the week. They also have schools where young people can learn about the faith and the history of the Jewish people.

## Learning about religion

❶ Make a list of the differences between Orthodox and Reform synagogues.

❷ 'Religions must always try to keep up-to-date.' How would an Orthodox Jew reply to this?

❸ Design a leaflet to explain what Reform Jews believe.

## Learning from religion

❶ 'You cannot change traditions without losing the meaning of the religion.' What do you think?

❷ 'Men and women are different and they need to be treated in different ways.' Comment.

# The Written Torah

In this section you will:

- think about how books influence your own lives
- learn about some of the important writings that Jews refer to for help in their lives and worship.

## The power of books

Ray Bradbury wrote a book called *Fahrenheit 451*. This was a fictional story about a time when a government burned books because it was afraid of the power they had to make people think for themselves.

*Reading the Torah at the Western Wall*

## Scriptures

Scripture is the name given to the writings of religions. They are important to people because they are about the events, people and teachings that are central to their beliefs.

Jews believe their holy writings, especially the **Torah**, teach the way God would like them to live.

## The Torah

'Blessed art Thou, O Lord God of the Universe, who hast chosen us from all people and hast given us thy Torah.'

This is the blessing said before the reading from the Torah in the **synagogue**.

Torah is the name given to the five books of Genesis, Exodus, Leviticus, Numbers and Deuteronomy.

The Torah contains stories of creation, the early leaders of the Jews and the story of Moses and the escape from Egypt. The Torah also contains the 613 **mitzvot** (rules) that were given to Moses. The Ten Commandments are included in the 613 mitzvot.

There are 248 positive and 365 negative mitzvot. The prayer robe often has 613 strands to remind Jews of these rules.

It is hard to remember so many rules. Some rules are not clear. Over the years, **rabbis** and teachers have discussed the meanings. One teacher was Rabbi Hillel in the first century CE. He wrote:

'What is hateful to you, do not do to your neighbour. That is the whole of the Torah. All else is commentary.'

Many Jewish children attend **cheder**, a school for the study of Torah. Some may go on to enter **Yeshiva**, a college for more advanced study.

**Orthodox** Jews believe that the Torah is the word of God and cannot be changed. Other Jews believe that it is all right to interpret the writings to fit in with modern life. For example, non-Orthodox Jews may not observe the **kosher** food laws or they may allow a woman to become a **rabbi**.

# Nevi'im and Ketuvim

Jews use the word 'Torah' to mean:

- the first five books of the Bible
- the whole of the **Tenakh** (the Written Torah)
- the later teachings that explain the Tenakh (the Oral Torah)

The other two parts of the Tenakh are called **Nevi'im** and **Ketuvim**.

The Nevi'im contain the historical books about the Kings of Israel and the writings of the prophets such as Isaiah.

The Ketuvim are books of poetry, songs and wise sayings, and includes the Psalms, Proverbs and the story of Job.

## Learning about religion

❶ Draw a diagram to show the holy writings that form the Tenakh.

❷ What do you think Rabbi Hillel meant by what he said about 'the whole Torah'?

❸ What are the main differences in the views held by Jews about the Torah?

## Learning from religion

❶ Can words written thousands of years ago still be relevant to people in the world today? Give reasons for your answers.

❷ How have you been influenced by books and films? Have they changed the way you look at the world in any way?

# The Oral Torah

## How is law made?

Law is always changing. Parliament makes laws, and courts have to uphold these laws.

However, sometimes courts have to apply laws to particular cases. The court may have to take into account aspects that the lawmakers did not consider.

Jewish scriptures have developed in similar ways.

First came the **mitzvot** in the **Tenakh**. Then, if the teachings of the Tenakh are too hard to understand, Jews have other writings that explain the Tenakh. As well as the Written **Torah** (the Tenakh) they can turn to the Oral Torah. This is a collection of the ideas of scholars and rabbis that try to make these laws clear.

*A law court in action*

## The Mishnah

The word **Mishnah** is Hebrew for 'to repeat, to study'. The Mishnah is the written version of the Oral Torah. It was written down in about 200 CE. It deals with things such as when to plant seeds, and how to prepare for and observe **Shabbat** and other festivals. It has sections about marriage, divorce, buying and selling, legal matters, sacrifices and the rules about purity.

**Rabbi** Judah the Prince collected and carefully edited these sayings.

## The Talmud

The **Talmud** took over 800 years to complete. It includes ideas of over 2000 Jewish teachers and rabbis. There are stories to help people to understand how to live, called **agadah**, which means 'telling'. There are halakhot (singular **halakhah**). These are teachings about how ancient laws can apply to new problems.

The Talmud contains some wise sayings such as:

- the health of the body depends upon the teeth
- charity knows no race or creed
- breakfast is the most important meal of the day.

## The Midrash

**Midrashim** are writings based on stories from the Tenakh, and the agadah. The writers often used examples from real life to explain the difficult parts of the Tenakh.

## How are these holy writings used today?

Jewish people refer to the Talmud, the Mishnah and the Midrash to help them to understand the meaning of the Written Torah. They do this to help them to put these teachings into practice. Judges in the Rabbinical courts (called **Bet Din**) may use them in divorce or inheritance cases.

### Learning about religion

❶ Why do you think Jewish people felt they needed the Mishnah and the Talmud?

❷ 'It is impossible to apply the Torah today.' How might a Jew reply to that statement?

### Learning from religion

❶ Choose one of the wise sayings based on the Talmud. Ask two people to speak for the statement and against the statement. Then vote for and against the statement.

❷ 'Your conscience will tell you how to live a good life, not a book.' How might a Jewish person answer this? What do you think? Give reasons for your answer.

# *Festivals 1 – Yom Kippur*

In this section you will:

● learn about the importance of **Yom Kippur** to Jewish people

● think about when it is right to forgive people and about what it means to be forgiven.

## Times to celebrate, times to think

Festivals help religious people to think about important aspects of their faith. Festivals can also help us to find answers to some important questions people ask. These questions are about how people ought to behave and what matters most in life.

## I can't forgive myself…

Have you ever done something that made you feel really guilty? Perhaps you did or said something cruel or nasty. Did you find it hard to forgive yourself?

*We all need to forgive ourselves sometimes*

Jews believe that justice and forgiveness go together.

At Yom Kippur, Jews ask God and other human beings to forgive them.

## What is Yom Kippur?

Yom Kippur means 'the Day of **Atonement**'. Atonement means to put right what you have done wrong in a practical way. On Yom Kippur, Jews also try to put things right with God. To do this, they know they have to ask God to forgive them, and to promise to change what is wrong with their lives.

**Rosh Hashanah** is Jewish New Year, and it falls in September or October. At this time, Jews remember God as creator. For ten days after New Year, the 'Days of Return', they make an effort to put things right that they have done wrong. Then on Yom Kippur, they remember God as Judge.

For a month before Yom Kippur, Jews hear the **shofar**, a ram's horn, as it is blown in the **synagogue**. This reminds them they need to ask for forgiveness. They also need to **repent**, that is, to turn away from their wrong ways, and turn back to God.

'On the tenth day of the seventh month, you must fast.'

Leviticus 16: 29

To **fast** is to give up food for a religious reason.

The day before Yom Kippur, Jews prepare themselves. They may use the **mikveh**, a special bath used to purify themselves.

They then eat their last meal before beginning a twenty-five hour fast.

*'To know what it is to be hungry, even for a single day, encourages pity for the hungry, the oppressed and the unfortunate.'*

Louis Jacobs, Jewish thinker

On Yom Kippur, Jews avoid sexual intercourse. They do not wear leather shoes. People used to think wearing leather shoes was showing off their wealth.

They spend the day in prayer, and try to settle any arguments they have with other people.

At the end of Yom Kippur, there is a service in the synagogue. They see the doors of the **Aron Hakodesh** (Ark) open wide. This is a way of saying that God wants to accept them. They hear the shofar once more, to signal the end of the day.

*Blowing the shofar*

## Learning about religion

❶ Write down the meanings of atonement, fasting and repentance.

❷ What are the most important events at Yom Kippur?

❸ Why do you think many Jews feel that Yom Kippur is the holiest day of the year?

## Learning from religion

❶ Is it always right to forgive other people? Give reasons for your answer.

❷ What would you find most difficult to give up for a day? Why?

❸ 'If Yom Kippur really worked, it wouldn't need to happen every year.' What do you think?

# Festivals 2 – Purim

In this section you will:
- learn why the festival of **Purim** is important to Jews
- think about how important it is to be true to your beliefs.

## The festival story

You can find the story of Purim in the book of Esther.

Many years ago, the Persian army invaded Israel. They took some Jews to their capital city, Susa. Two of the captives were Esther and her cousin, Mordecai.

One day, the King of Persia, Xerxes, ordered his wife, Queen Vashti, to come to a party. She refused. The King was angry. His advisers told him he should divorce her before anyone heard about what she had done.

The King's prime minister, Haman, set out to find a new queen.

*Jewish children performing a Purim play*

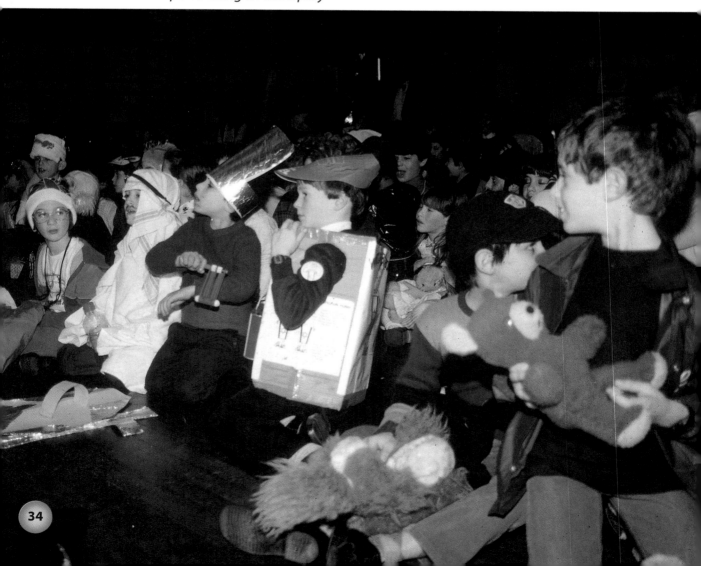

Among the girls taken to the King's palace was Esther. Mordecai told Esther she must not let the king know that she was a Jew.

King Xerxes thought Esther was the most beautiful of all the girls, and he married her.

Haman hated the Jews, especially Mordecai, and planned to kill them. He drew lots (like a lottery) to see what day he would murder Mordecai and the rest of the Jews.

Mordecai heard about Haman's plot. He asked Esther to talk to the King while in his private room. Women were not allowed to approach the king, on pain of death. Esther was not afraid. She told the King she was Jewish, and about Haman's plot.

The King was angry with Haman. That night, at dinner, he told Haman he knew Esther was Jewish and that he knew about his plan. He ordered his guard to hang Haman on the gallows he had built for Mordecai. The Jews were saved.

After this, Haman's friends were punished, and the Jews were allowed to defend themselves against attack.

## Purim today

Purim is the name for 'lots' and this gave the festival its name.

The festival of Purim begins with the reading of the story of Esther in the **synagogue**. This continues into the next day.

Children often dress up and perform plays based on the story. Whenever Haman's name is mentioned, children 'boo' loudly or stamp their feet. They may wave a **greggar** (a rattle) to try and stop the name being heard.

The **Talmud** says people should give presents at Purim. People often give two items of food to friends. Some, however, send a book.

Most **Orthodox** Jews believe the events of Purim happened as the book of Esther records them. Many **Reform** Jews are less sure, as there is no other historical record of this story. However, both agree that this story shows how God saves those who trust in Him.

### Learning about religion

❶ Why do you think Purim is still important for Jews today?

❷ Does it matter if the story of Purim did not happen exactly as the book of Esther tells it? Give reasons for your answer.

❸ Draw a picture strip to illustrate the story of Esther.

### Learning from religion

❶ Haman tried to get rid of the Jews because he was racist. What do you think causes racism? Give as many reasons as possible.

❷ Part of the story of Esther is about revenge (Haman hanging instead of Mordecai). Is revenge ever right? Why might religious people think it wrong?

# The Western Wall

In this section you will:
● learn about the Western Wall and why it is important to Jews
● think about the importance of places to peoples' religious faith.

## The journey of life

Life is like a journey. But does this journey of life have a reason? Or is it just the fun of travelling that matters?

For religious people, making a journey to visit a place that is important to their faith helps them to focus on this faith.

## Tale of a temple

When the ancestors of the Jews first began to worship God, they would gather rocks together to mark the place. By the time of Moses, they worshipped in a large tent called the Tabernacle.

Within the Tabernacle was a special area called the Holy of Holies. Inside, there was a box called the **Ark of the Covenant**.

According to the **Tenakh**, this contained two tablets of stone. These were the stones bearing the Ten Commandments that God gave to Moses.

The Tenakh says that King David made Jerusalem his capital city. His son, Solomon, built a temple there.

The temple became the centre for Jewish religion. This was because the Ark of the Covenant, within the Holy of Holies, was so sacred that only the High Priest could visit it on one day in the year.

Secondly, animals were sacrificed in the temple as a way of saying sorry to God for the bad things the people had done, or saying thank you for the good things that God had done for the people.

Invaders destroyed the temple of Solomon. Then it was re-built. Later, invaders also destroyed the second temple.

At the beginning of the first century CE, King Herod had just built a new temple.

In 66 CE, the Jews rebelled against the Romans, who ruled the land at that time. In 70 CE, the Romans set fire to Jerusalem and destroyed the temple, apart from the Western Wall.

## The Western Wall today

The Western Wall still stands in the centre of Jerusalem. For many Jews it is a symbol of their hope that one day a new temple will be built there. Many Jews go there to pray.

Today, the Wall is like an open-air synagogue. Men and women stand separately, as they do in an **Orthodox synagogue**. Men wear **kippot** to cover their heads while they pray. Some parents may hold a son's **Bar Mitzvah** there.

Some people write a prayer on paper and place it in a gap in the wall. These pieces of paper have to be removed from time to time.

When the State of Israel was founded in 1948, the Western Wall was in the part of Jerusalem that belonged to the Arab country of Jordan. Above the wall on a hill are the Muslim holy places of the Dome of the Rock and the Black Mosque. In 1967, there was a war and Israel captured the area round the Western Wall. This made it easier for Jews to visit this important site.

### Learning about religion

❶ Draw a series of pictures to show how Jews have worshipped (stone altars, the Tabernacle, the temple, and so on).

❷ Why is the Western Wall important to Jews today?

❸ Working in a small group, use CD-ROMs, the Internet or books to find out more about the area round the Western Wall. Prepare a short talk or a wall feature for your classroom.

### Learning from religion

❶ What places are important to you? Explain why they are important.

❷ What prayers would you write on paper to put between the stones of the Western Wall? Give reasons for your answer.

# *Masada*

## Dying for what you believe in?

There are many examples in history where people have preferred to die rather than give up their religion.

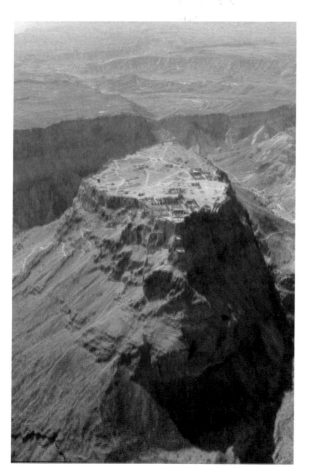

*Masada made an impressive fortress*

## Masada today

Masada is a hill, about 150 metres high, that rises out of the desert near the Dead Sea in Israel. It is very hot there – often over 40° centigrade. People usually ride up to the top on a cable-car, rather than try to walk up the rocky path.

Archaeologists uncovered the site of Masada in the 1960s. Since then many travellers have visited it. Soldiers in the Israeli army have to run from the bottom of the hill to the top in full kit. Then they promise, 'Masada will not fall again!'

## Why Masada became important

In 4 BCE, King Herod the Great built his palace on top of Masada. After his death, the Romans took control of it for a time.

In 66 CE, a Jewish group called the **Zealots** started a civil war against the Romans. One part of this group captured Masada and made it their base. Several families lived there.

In 72 CE, the Romans decided to deal with the Zealots. On Masada the Zealots grew food and had a water supply, and stores of food that would last many years. How could the Romans get the Jews off this hill?

They set up camp round the base of Masada. They put up fences so that no-one could get in or out. They brought an army of slaves to build a ramp up to the fort at the top of the hill. After many months, the Romans reached the top.

*The Romans stormed Masada*

The leader of the Zealots, Eleazar, told them it was better to die as free people than to be slaves of the Romans. They chose ten men to kill the nine hundred and sixty people who lived there. They set the fortress alight. Then they killed themselves.

When the Romans broke through the walls, they found their enemies dead. Not all the inhabitants died. Two women and five children hid in order to avoid being killed. According to the historian, Josephus, they told the Romans the story of what had happened.

The Romans were impressed by the actions of the Zealots. They also believed it was better to die than to suffer dishonour.

It seemed that in a way it was the Zealots who had won the battle of Masada.

The battle for Masada was just one small conflict in a terrible time for the Jews. Thousands died or lost their homes. Many were taken as slaves to Rome, and had to fight as gladiators in the arena.

## Learning about religion

❶ What do you think the Israeli soldiers mean by the vow 'Masada shall not fall again'?

❷ Imagine you were a survivor of Masada. Write an account of why the people chose to die. Remember to include what Eleazar said to them.

❸ Why do you think many modern Jews visit Masada today?

## Learning from religion

❶ Do you think the people on Masada were right to do what they did? Give reasons for your answer.

❷ A martyr is someone who dies for the sake of their religion. Using the school library, CD-ROMs or other resources, find out about other religious martyrs. Choose one and write a short paragraph about him or her.

39

# Circumcision – sign of the covenant

In this section you will:
- learn about **circumcision** and why it is important to many Jews
- think about the birth of children and welcoming new life.

*A new life*

## Stages of life

All through your life there have been special moments. When you were born the people who love you may have had a party. When you left primary school there may have been a final assembly.

Religious people have special ways of celebrating the important moments in life. They have naming ceremonies for new babies. There are 'coming of age' celebrations, and weddings. These special celebrations are called **rites of passage**.

## The covenant promise

The birth of a new baby boy or girl is a very happy moment for a Jewish family. Boys have a special ceremony to welcome them into the Jewish community. This is called circumcision.

Circumcision is the removing of the foreskin from a boy's penis. People practised this in ancient times, before Judaism was a faith. Members of some other religions carry it out today. For Jews it is a sign of their **covenant** with God.

Jewish people call the ceremony **Brit Milah**, the 'covenant of circumcision'. It links to the first circumcision that Abraham performed as a sign of this covenant. Here is one of the prayers used at the ceremony:

'Praised be thou, O Lord our God, ruling Spirit of the Universe, who has commanded us to enter into the Covenant of our father Abraham.'

Jewish Prayer Book

Circumcision takes place on the eighth day after the mother has given birth. It can take place in the **synagogue** or in the home of the baby's family. At the synagogue, it happens after morning prayers.

The man who performs the circumcision is called the **mohel**. He is specially trained to do this.

Many Jews believe the spirit of the prophet Elijah is present at every circumcision. There is a special chair – Elijah's Chair. The mohel puts the baby on the chair for a moment, then he gives the baby to the **sandek**.

*A party to celebrate a new birth*

The sandek is usually one of the baby's grandfathers. He holds the baby on his lap while the operation takes place.

The father recites a special blessing for his son, and the mohel announces the baby's Hebrew name. Most babies have an English name as well.

The whole group now prays that the newly circumcised boy will faithfully follow the **Torah** and be a good person. There is wine for all to drink, and a party to celebrate the life of a new child.

The family takes the foreskin away and buries it as a mark of respect.

Nearly all Jewish boys are circumcised. When the **Reform** Movement began, they asked whether they should continue this practice. However, most decided it was too important to be left out of Jewish rites of passage.

There is also a special naming ceremony for girls. This takes place when they are thirty days old.

## Learning about religion

❶ Who are the mohel and the sandek? Why are they important in the Brit Milah ceremony?

❷ Why are Abraham and Elijah important in this ceremony?

❸ Use books, CD-ROMs and the Internet to find out about the ceremony to welcome Jewish girls into the community. Write down what you find.

## Learning from religion

❶ What promises do you think parents should make to their child? Think of three and give reasons for your choices.

❷ Even people who are not religious like to have a public naming ceremony. Why do you think this is?

# *Becoming an adult*

## When are you a grown-up?

The French writer Victor Hugo wrote about two people that 'one got older, the other matured'.

When is a person an adult? Is this different from being mature?

British law sets different ages for being mature. You can be held responsible for a crime at ten, drive a car at seventeen, and are allowed to vote at eighteen.

Who matures more quickly? Boys or girls? Most people will regard you as adult when you are responsible.

For Jews, when boys and girls become adult, and full members of their religion they are called Bar Mitzvah or Bat Mitzvah.

## Bar Mitzvah

Bar Mitzvah means 'Son of the Commandment'. It is the point at which a boy becomes an adult member of the Jewish community.

He will wear a **tallit** and learn to put on the **tefillin**.

Being Bar Mitzvah does not depend on having a ceremony, but most boys do. This takes place on the **Shabbat** after the boy's thirteenth birthday. He has to learn Hebrew and practise reading the portion of the **Torah** that he has to read in the service. A **rabbi** helps him to do this.

His father says a blessing as he steps up to read.

After the reading, there is usually a special meal to celebrate his Bar Mitzvah. He may make a little speech, thanking his parents and promising to keep the faith.

He is now a full member of the **synagogue**. He can be part of the **minyan**. He is now old enough to keep the fast on **Yom Kippur**.

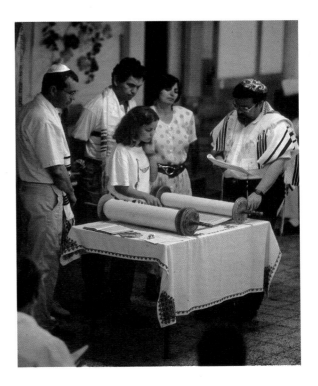

## Bat Mitzvah

**Reform** Jews decided that girls should also have a ceremony to mark their adulthood. This is Bat Mitzvah, which means 'Daughter of the Commandment'. It happens when a girl is twelve. She learns about keeping Shabbat and festivals. She may also read from the Torah.

**Orthodox** Jews may have a ceremony called **Bat Chayil**, 'Daughter of Worth'. This may take place on a Sunday, rather than Shabbat. She will not read from the Torah, but may read from another part of the **Tenakh**.

### Learning about religion

❶ Write a letter to a friend who was not able to attend your Bar or Bat Mitzvah. Describe what happened and how you felt.

❷ Why do you think these ceremonies are important to Jewish people?

### Learning from religion

❶ What do you think are the differences between getting older and becoming mature?

❷ Jews consider boys and girls mature at different ages. Do you agree? Give reasons for your answer.

# Getting married

## Why get married?

What sort of person would you like to marry?

Many people today decide to live together without being married. However, people do still have a marriage ceremony. Why?

Religious people may want to make their promises in front of God and their religious community. Others may want to state publicly their love for each other.

*Marriage is about commitment*

## The Jewish wedding ceremony

Most Jewish families are happy if their children marry other Jews. This is because they will bring up their children in the faith and there is no conflict. A child born of a Jewish mother is Jewish. If a Jewish man 'marries out' this can cause problems within the family.

Some Jews might encourage the non-Jewish partner to convert to Judaism. They may ask them to promise they will bring up their children in the Jewish faith.

In Hebrew, marriage is called **kiddushin**, which means 'holy', as Jews believe marriage is holy.

Before the wedding, the bridegroom signs a marriage contract, the **Ketubah**. In it, he promises to take care of his wife.

The marriage can take place on any day except **Shabbat**, and may be held in the **synagogue**. The bride, groom and witnesses stand under a **huppah**, a canopy on four poles.

The **rabbi** conducts the ceremony, but a **cantor** may sing the blessings. The first blessing welcomes the bride and groom:

'Blessed is the one who comes in the name of the Lord.'

The huppah stands for the new home the couple will make together.

The bride and groom take a sip of wine from the same glass. The groom then places a ring on the right hand forefinger of his bride and says a blessing. He may read out the promises he has made in the Ketubah. The cantor will then sing seven blessings for the couple.

The bridegroom then takes the wine glass and wraps it in cloth. He places it on the floor and stamps on it. This is a symbolic act. It says that marriage will have to face bad times as well as good. It also reminds them that the temple in Jerusalem was destroyed and has never been re-built.

After the formal ceremony, there is a wedding reception. Since no marriages are allowed on Shabbat, Sundays and Tuesdays are the most popular days for this ceremony.

## Learning about religion

❶ Write an email about a wedding in your family, as if you were a Jewish child writing to a non-Jewish friend. Explain the important parts of the ceremony.

❷ Why do you think the Ketubah is important to the marriage?

## Learning from religion

❶ All wedding ceremonies have vows (promises) between the bride and groom. What vows would you like your partner to make if you get married? Give reasons for your answer.

❷ 'Marriage is out-of-date.' Organize a class debate on this subject.

*The bridal party meet under the huppah*

# Death

In this section you will:
- learn about Jewish ideas concerning death and mourning
- think about your own ideas about what happens when we die.

## Ultimate statistic

The writer George Bernard Shaw said that death is the ultimate statistic: every one of us dies!

We all have to face the fact that we will die. How does religion help people face death? Does religion help us to think about the really important question: is this life all there is?

*A Jewish graveyard*

## Jewish funerals

A truly observant Jew, if they know they are about to die, tries to recite the **Shema** and to ask God to forgive their sins.

**Orthodox** Jews insist that their dead must be buried, though **Reform** Jews may allow cremation. The funeral takes place, if possible, within twenty-four hours of the death.

As soon as the family hears of the death of a loved one, they make small tears in their clothes, as a sign of their grief.

A close relative prepares the body for burial. They wash the body and wrap it in a plain linen shroud (burial cloth). Men may be wrapped in their **tallit**.

As the body is lowered into the ground, the **rabbi** recites the **kaddish**, a special prayer for mourning and remembrance.

May God's great name be blessed, forever and ever.

May God's name be blessed, praised, glorified, revered, held in awe, acclaimed and revered – though it is higher than all the blessings, songs, praises and consolations that can be spoken in this world.

May Heaven grant a universal peace and life for us and for all Israel, Amen.

Extract from the kaddish

# Mourning

**Judaism** encourages people who have lost a loved one to grieve.

For the first week, the family sits **shiva**. The word means 'seven'. The close family members stay at home and others visit them. They offer comfort, and pray with the family. Traditionally, the mourners sit on low chairs during this week. This symbolizes that the whole body is 'brought low' by grief. Male mourners recite kaddish.

For the month after the funeral, there is **sheloshin**, which means 'thirty'. Male mourners visit the **synagogue** every day to recite kaddish. After this, things begin to return to normal, although observant Jews will not go to parties for a year after the death of a close relative, out of respect.

The third stage is **Yahrzeit** ('year-time'). On the first anniversary of the death, a Jewish family lights a candle. This remembers the verse from Proverbs,

'A person's soul is the candle of the Lord.' They give thanks to God for the life of the one who has died. Close family members will hold Yahrzeit every year on the anniversary of the death of their loved one.

Jews may have a gravestone with the person's name engraved on it. It is a tradition to place small stones on the grave at each visit. Abraham marked Sarah's grave like this.

Jews believe that God will reward a person who has led a good life. God will also judge the wicked. Jews believe that the 'after life' is in the hands of God, and not something to think about now.

## Learning about religion

❶ Choose three Jewish symbols of mourning. Explain what they mean.

❷ How do Jewish traditions help people to come to terms with the death of a close relative?

❸ What effect might Jewish beliefs about God's judgement have on a Jew's life?

## Learning from religion

❶ Should funerals be simple or grand? Give reasons for your answer.

❷ What do you think happens after people die? Give reasons for your answer.

# God's world or ours?

## Tu B'Shvat

Tu B'Shvat is the festival of tree planting – a 'New Year for Trees'. It comes at the end of the harvest. In Israel, people try to plant new trees as a sign that they are willing to give back to the land as well as to take from it.

## The Torah on animals

Jews believe that the seven laws given to Noah, The **Noachide Laws**, apply to all people (see page 50). The fourth of these laws is 'Be kind to animals'.

The **Torah** also encourages Jewish people to help animals:

'If you see your friend's ass or his ox has fallen on the road, you must help him raise it.'

Deuteronomy 22: 4

## A balance of nature

A **rabbi** once said 'The world follows its own habit'. This means that God intended that there should be balances in nature.

Jews believe that it is their responsibility to keep this balance.

*Planting trees is a sign of hope and thankfulness*

*Noah's Ark*

God is the creator. Human beings are his stewards. It is their task to look after things and not spoil the world for future generations.

## The rowing boat

Some people use the story of Noah as a story with a meaning. It means that if you want to be obedient to God, one way is to show that you care for the environment. This is what Noah did when he obeyed God's call to rescue the animals.

A group of Jewish teachers said people should think about the environment in this way: we have a responsibility to life. We must protect it. This world is like a great ark (boat) and we are all passengers in it. This world is fragile, and we must work together to protect it.

### Learning about religion

❶ Why do you think one of the seven Noachide Laws forbids cruelty to animals?

❷ What do you think it means to be a 'steward' of God's creation?

### Learning from religion

❶ Write two lists of things that humans do that are good for the earth or that damage the earth.

❷ Should every country have a regular tree planting ceremony? Give reasons for your answer.

# Creation and the environment

In this section you will:
- learn about the Jewish idea of creation
- think about where human life comes from and its value to the world.

## What a wonderful world

Have you ever seen something of such beauty that you felt deep emotion? Or had a personal experience that has really moved you? Everyone can experience a sense of wonder – not just religious people.

Religious people may find these experiences make them think about what matters most. Jewish people may reflect on the idea of God as a creator.

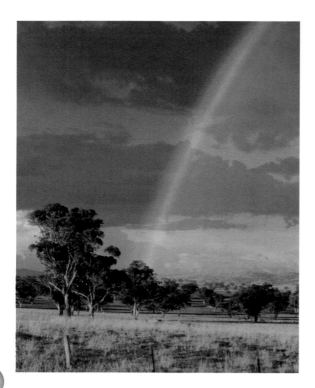

## The Noachide Laws

Jews believe that everyone, Jewish or not, should follow the laws that God gave to Noah after the flood.

1. Do not worship **idols**.
2. Do not murder.
3. Do not steal.
4. Avoid sexual misconduct.
5. Be kind to animals.
6. Avoid blasphemy.
7. Worship only one God.

## Creation

The **Torah** teaches that God is the creator, and that all that exists comes from God.

The story of creation in Genesis says that God created the world in six days, and rested on the seventh day. Some people believe that this is literally true. Others believe the story is not about *how* God created the world, but *why*.

At the end of each day of creation, the Torah says, 'God saw that it was very good.' Jewish people believe that God gave human beings a special trust to care for the planet. Humans are responsible if things go wrong.

'God blessed them [man and woman] and said "Be fruitful and increase; fill the earth and subdue it; have dominion over the fish in the sea, the birds of the air and every living thing that moves on the earth."'

Genesis 1: 28

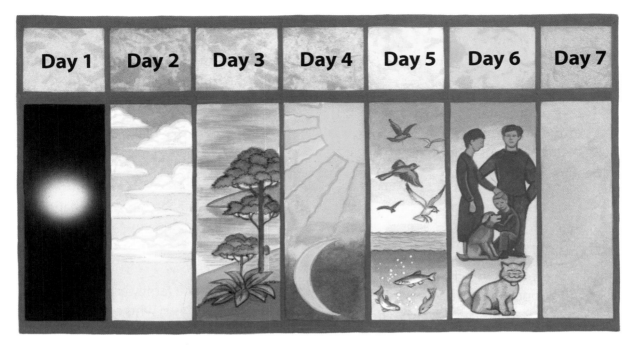

| Day 1 | Day 2 | Day 3 | Day 4 | Day 5 | Day 6 | Day 7 |

*The Genesis creation calendar*

'The heavens show the glory of God, the sky makes known his handiwork.'

Psalm 19: 1

In the past, many Jews thought this meant that human beings could use the environment how they saw fit. Now, most Jews would say that humans must work with God to care for the world about them.

There are ideas in the Torah about caring for and improving the world. For example, **Shabbat** is a rest for animals as well as people. The earth must 'rest' for a year after every seven years, so that it is refreshed.

Even armies must take care:

'When in your war against a city you have to besiege it for a long time in order to capture it, you must not destroy its trees…You may eat (the fruit) of them, but you must not cut them down.'

Deuteronomy 20: 19

## Learning about religion

❶ Why do you think the Jewish faith has a creation story?

❷ Design a diagram to show the different ways of understanding the creation story.

❸ Do you think the ideas of creation might have led to problems for the environment as well as protection? Explain your answer.

## Learning from religion

❶ Design a poster to explain some of the major environmental problems we face today.

❷ Have you ever had a sense of wonder? Write a poem to show what this was like for you.

In this section you will:
● learn about Jewish beliefs concerning money, family and drugs, and how their beliefs affect their behaviour
● think about your own attitude to these issues.

## Morality

Morality has to do with choosing between right and wrong. Some people think that their conscience tells them what to do. Others, especially religious people, think that you can find out what God wants you to do by turning to the scriptures.

## Money

Many Jews have a small collection box in their homes called **pushkes**. They give money regularly to charities such as Jewish Care, which looks after the elderly and disabled.

The Ten Commandments warn people not to steal, or even to want things that are not theirs. There are many teachings about wealth:

'Be wise enough not to wear yourself out trying to get rich.'

Proverbs 23: 7

'Since there will never cease to be some in need on the earth, I therefore command you, "Open your hand to the poor and needy neighbour in your land."'

Deuteronomy 15: 11

The **Talmud** (see page 31) tells how being poor is a miserable state, and people should help others to escape poverty.

## Family life

'Honour your father and your mother so that your days may be long in the land that the Lord is giving you.'

Exodus 20: 12

Jews believe that a family is an important part of society. This is where people learn to love one another and where children receive their first education. Jews believe children should care for their parents when they become older.

Jews also see the family as an important place where the religion is passed on.

*Family life is important to Jewish people*

This is where children learn about the important festivals, the food laws, and other aspects of what it means to be Jewish.

Parents are responsible for bringing up their children properly. The Talmud advises: 'Teach your son a trade or you teach him to become a robber.'

Marriage is important to Jews. It is within marriage that two people develop and become fully mature. Only in rare cases does a divorce take place.

## Alcohol

Jews are allowed to drink alcohol. They use wine in religious ceremonies. However, they do not approve of heavy drinking. The **Midrash** says, 'Wine enters, sense goes out; wine enters, secrets come out.'

Jewish judges are not allowed to pass judgement if they have drunk even one glass of wine. They must wait until the alcohol has passed from their body.

## Drugs

Jews believe that drugs should only be used for medical reasons. Many Jews campaign against the misuse of drugs.

They believe that human beings are made 'in the image of God'. Hence they must care for their bodies in a responsible way.

*Drugs can bring all kinds of problems*

### Learning about religion

❶ Find out about one of the
following Jewish charities: Jewish Care, Norwood Child Care or Chai-Lifeline. Use a CD-ROM, books or the Internet. Write a short article about it for your school magazine.

❷ What might a Jewish teenager think about their traditional family life?

### Learning from religion

❶ What could you do to help people in need?

❷ Family life has changed in the last half-century. Does the Jewish teaching about family life still have meaning? Explain your answer.

# Why is there suffering?

In this section you will:

● learn how Jewish people have suffered anti-Semitism

● think about **scapegoating** and how this is part of anti-Semitism.

## Scapegoating

Sometimes particular people are picked on or bullied, when others are left alone. Maybe it is because of the colour of their hair, or because they wear glasses, or speak differently or have a different colour skin.

Sometimes one group of people picks on another, smaller group and blames them for everything that is bad in their own lives. This can be called scapegoating.

It is named after a practice the ancestors of the Jews used to do when they lived in deserts. A priest would choose a goat, and recite over the goat's head all the sins of the people. They drove the goat out into the desert to take away the sins from the people.

People today use scapegoats to take away their anger or sense of failure.

## Jewish suffering before the Holocaust

In 70 CE, the Romans destroyed the temple in Jerusalem. They forced Jews to leave Israel. The Jews went to live in countries in North Africa and Europe. This event is known as the **diaspora**, which means 'scattering'.

When the Roman Empire became Christian, this led to problems for many Jews.

People were prejudiced against Jews. Christians often thought this was justified, because, they said, Jews had allowed Jesus to be crucified. Jesus was Jewish, but those who hated Jews ignored this important fact.

In 1066 CE, there were Jews in England. The Christian church did not allow its members to be money-lenders. They forced Jews to do this.

In 1290 CE, King Edward expelled Jews from England. They were not allowed to return until the seventeenth century.

In Europe, many people attacked Jews. In Russia the Tsars (rulers in Russia) encouraged the army to attack Jews. Over a million Jews left Russia in the 1880s CE. Non-Jewish Russians helped the Tsar's army to persecute Jews. They drove them away from their homes and destroyed their houses and their possessions.

Over 100,000 Russian and Polish Jews came to England and others went to the USA. They set up new businesses and schools.

## The scandal of Captain Dreyfus

In the 1890s CE, Captain Dreyfus, an army officer, was falsely accused of spying for Germany.

In the early twentieth century, many Jews began to move to the country of Palestine. They set up **kibbutzim** (communal farms) and built the city of Tel Aviv on land they bought from the local Arab people.

*Captain Alfred Dreyfus*

Dreyfus was Jewish. Many people thought that this was the reason why he was accused – not because there was any evidence against him.

Dreyfus was given a life sentence. However, many famous people campaigned and Dreyfus was eventually released.

A young Swiss journalist, Theodor Hertzl, wrote about the case. He said that as long as Jews lived in Europe, they would always be victims. They needed a country of their own. This would be the new Israel. The idea is called **Zionism**.

## Learning about religion

❶ What is scapegoating? Why did Jews suffer from it?

❷ Give two examples of Jewish suffering before the twentieth century.

❸ Find out more about the trial of Captain Dreyfus. Write a play about it.

## Learning from religion

❶ Use a CD-ROM or dictionary to find out what the following words mean: genocide, prejudice, discrimination, stereotypes. Carry out one of the following activities:

  a Write a paragraph about the meaning of each word.

  b Produce a poster of collage about one of the words, using examples from news items.

❷ Why are some people bullied more often than others? Give reasons for your answer.

# The Holocaust

## The Holocaust

'Holocaust' means 'burnt offering'. The word refers to the suffering of the Jews from 1933–45 in Europe. Adolf Hitler, leader of the Nazi Party in Germany, began by banning Jews from parks, theatres and universities. His Nazi Party organized book-burnings and attacks against Jewish businesses. At the start of World War II the Nazis set up **concentration camps**. They intended to kill all Jews in Europe.

## Escape from Sobibor

There were many concentration camps from which people had little hope of escaping. However, on 14 October 1943, over 300 Jews escaped from the camp of Sobibor. A quarter of a million Jews had been murdered there. Every day, trains arrived carrying thousands of people from Nazi-occupied Europe. As they got off the trains, they were divided into two groups.

Those who could work were taken to one side. Those who could not – older people, women with children – were taken to gas chambers and killed. It took about fifteen to twenty minutes to die.

A group of prisoners stole some weapons and killed their guards. Their leaders encouraged them to escape.

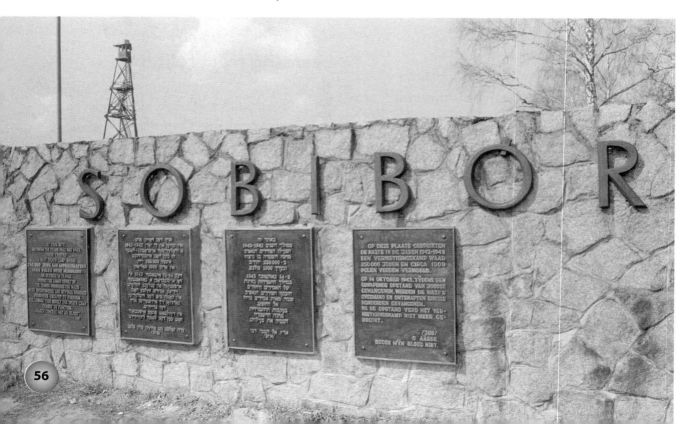

Over 600 prisoners rushed the gates and took on the other guards. Many were shot, and others died when they stepped on land-mines outside the camp. But about 300 managed to escape.

Some religious Jews refused to go, as they knew they would have to break the commandment 'You shall not kill'. For all that the Nazis had done to them, they did not believe it was right to fight back.

After the escape, the Nazis closed the camp and buried it. Now, in the woods around Sobibor, there is a statue in memory of those who died there. It has the words 'Never Again' carved in the stone.

The concentration camps were so awful that many Jews stopped believing in a God of love. Others became religious, as they came to believe that there had to be One who was better than human beings.

The Chief **Rabbi**, Dr Jonathan Sacks, wrote:

'We will never understand the Holocaust. But the asking of questions is itself a religious act. Future generations will ask: Why do we keep on being Jews? The answer is: To tell the story of our death sentence and our survival. And if they do not ask, we must make them ask.'

# God is hanging

Ellie Wiesel wrote a book about his time in a concentration camp. It is called *Night*. He tells this story:

'The SS hanged two Jewish men and a youth in front of the whole camp. The men died quickly, but the death throes of the youth lasted for half an hour.

'"Where is God? Where is he?" someone asked behind me.

'As the youth hung in torment in the noose after a long time, I heard a man call again, "Where is God now?"

'And I heard a voice in myself, "Where is he? He is hanging there on the gallows."'

## Learning about religion

❶ How did the Holocaust affect Jewish beliefs about God?

❷ Write a letter from a survivor of a camp like Sobibor to explain what life was like in the camp.

❸ What do you think Ellie Wiesel meant when he said that God was hanging on the gallows?

## Learning from religion

❶ Does suffering make it harder or easier to believe in a God of love?

❷ Should war criminals always be punished? Think of recent examples and write a paragraph to say what you think should happen.

# Does God exist?

In this section you will:

- learn more about Jewish ideas about God
- learn how that affects the way they live
- think about what religious beliefs show about human beings.

*Job's faith was tested by God*

## Does God exist?

'The fool says in his heart, "There is no God. Everyone is evil, every deed is bad, No one does any good!"'

Psalm 14: 1

Jews usually say that to be Jewish, you must believe in God. However, there are some Jews who follow some of the religious laws and festivals who do not believe in God.

The question for most Jews is not 'does God exist?', but 'what sort of being is God?'

A famous story tells how, in one of the **concentration camps**, some Jews put God on trial for ignoring their pain. They decided this God did not care. They found God 'guilty' of letting his people down. After the trial, they went off to worship the God they found guilty.

In the story in the **Tenakh**, Job has to learn that God alone is in control. He says,

'The Lord gives and the Lord takes away; Blessed be the name of the Lord.'

Job 1: 21

Jews believe that God cannot be proved or disproved by argument. God has to be experienced.

## What is God like?

Jews believe that God has always been there. God has no beginning and no end: God has always existed.

Jews believe that God created everything that exists out of nothing. God continues to create things. Human beings help in this work.

The **Shema** teaches that God is one. Jews believe that God is holy and God is good.

God is in control.

God cannot be represented by an image or an **idol**. The name of God is too holy to be known. Many Jewish books do not print the name of God. Even the word 'God' is represented 'G-D'.

Jews must only worship this one true God.

God is Spirit and is eternal. God knows everything that has happened and that will happen.

God is the Lord of History and makes things better. By giving the law through Moses and sending his messengers, the **prophets**, God shows that he cares for the world and the chosen people.

God is the one true judge. He punishes evil and rewards those who live as He wants them to live.

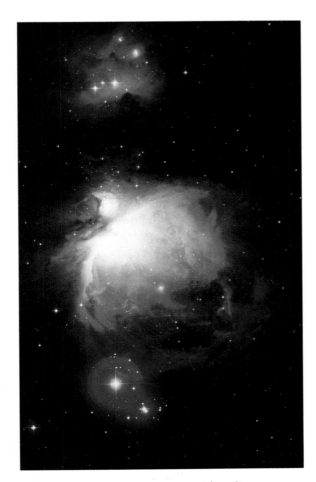

*The universe: creation or accident?*

## Learning about religion

❶ Write down the definitions of the following words: **atheist**, **agnostic** and **theist**. Which word applies to the way you believe? Why do you say this?

❷ Write two lists, headed, 'What God is' and 'What God does'. Use the information about Jewish beliefs on this page to complete the two lists.

❸ Do you think it is possible to be a Jew without believing in God? Give reasons for your answer.

## Learning from religion

❶ Choose any two Jewish beliefs about God and say how the world might be different if everyone shared these ideas.

❷ How might it influence people's actions if they believe that God knows what they are doing?

# Glossary

**Agadah**  stories in the Talmud to help people

**Agnostic**  someone who is not sure whether there is a God

**Amidah**  a prayer with eighteen blessings to God

**Aron Hakodesh/Ark of the Covenant**  the cupboard where the Torah and other scrolls are stored in the synagogue

**Ashkenazim**  Jews whose ancestors came from Central and Eastern Europe

**Atheist**  a person who believes there is no God

**Atonement**  being at one with God

**Bar Mitzvah**  'Son of the Commandment'; a boy who reaches Jewish adulthood at age thirteen

**Bat Chayil**  'Daughter of Excellence'; a ceremony for girls reaching the age of twelve

**Bat Mitzvah**  'Daughter of the Commandment'; a girl who reaches Jewish adulthood at age twelve

**Bet Din**  'House of Justice'; a Jewish court of law

**Bet ha Knesset**  'House of Assembly'; Hebrew name for a synagogue

**Bimah**  raised platform in a synagogue where the Torah is read

**Brit milah**  covenant of circumcision

**Challah**  (plural **-ot**) special plaited loaves of bread for Shabbat and festivals

**Cantor**  the person who leads prayers in the synagogue

**Cheder**  religion classes for Jewish children

**Circumcision**  removal of the foreskin from the penis for religious or health reasons

**Concentration camps**  camps organized by the Nazis in World War II for the extermination of Jews and other groups they disapproved of

**Covenant**  the promise made by God to care for the Jewish people

**Diaspora**  'dispersion'; the name given to Jews living outside Israel

**Exodus**  (1) the escape from Egypt led by Moses; (2) second book of the Torah

**Fast**  to go without food for a religious reason

**Genocide**  mass destruction of a whole race of people

**Greggar**  wooden rattle used whenever Haman's name is spoken in the telling of the story of Esther

**Halakhah**  the laws of Judaism

**Hanukiah**  eight-branched candlestick used at Hanukkah

**Hanukkah**  an eight-day festival of lights

**Havdalah**  'separation'; the ceremony marking the end of Shabbat

**Holocaust**  the murder of over six million Jews by Nazis in Europe 1933–45. Also knows as Shoah

**Huppah**  the canopy under which a Jewish couple are married

**Idol**  a statue worshipped as a god

**Judaism**  the religion of Jewish people

**Kaddish**  a prayer of praise to God said by a mourner

**Ketubah**  the marriage contract

**Ketuvim**  'writings'; the third section of the Tenakh

**Kibbutz**  a communal farm or settlement

**Kiddush**  prayer of blessing said at the beginning of Shabbat

**Kiddushin**  'sanctification'; a Jewish marriage

**Kippah**  head covering worn by Jews

**Knesset**  Israeli Parliament

**Kosher**  food that Jews are allowed to eat

**Magen David Adom**  'Shield of David'; a six-pointed star emblem

**Manna**  bread provided for the Israelites when they escaped from Egypt

**Menorah**  six-branched candlestick

**Messiah**  'the anointed one of God'; a king-like figure who God will send at the end of time

**Mezuzah**  a miniature scroll in a case, fixed to the right door-post of Jewish homes

**Midrash**  a collection of commentaries on the Tenakh

**Mikveh**  pool for Jewish ritual bathing

**Minyan**  minimum number of adults needed for public worship, usually ten

**Miracle**  an act of God that suspends the laws of nature

**Mishnah**  Jewish religious books, collection of teachings of the rabbis

**Mitzvot**  'commandments'; Jewish religious laws; good deeds

**Mohel**  person who performs circumcisions

**Monotheism**  belief in the existence of only one God

**Ner Tamid**  the eternal light kept burning in a synagogue

**Nevi'im**  the writings of the prophets and historical books in the Tenakh

**Noachide Laws**  the seven laws given to Noah that Jews regard as basic rules for morality for all human beings

**Oral law**  teachings based on the laws in the Torah, later written down in the Mishnah and the Talmud

**Orthodox Jews**  Jews who observe traditional Jewish teachings and uphold Orthodoxy

**Patriarch**  founding father of a religion

**Pesach**  Hebrew for Passover; festival to remind Jews how God rescued them from slavery in Egypt

**Prophet**  messenger of God

**Purim**  festival to remember how Esther rescued the Jews from death

**Pushkes**  charity collection box in a Jewish home

**Rabbi**  spiritual leader and teacher in a Jewish community

**Reform Jews**  Jews who felt that Judaism had to change to fit in with modern society

**Repent**  be sorry and try to change the way you live

**Rites of passage**  special ceremonies that mark an important event in life such as birth or marriage

**Rosh Hashanah**  Jewish New Year

**Sandek**  the person who holds a baby boy at his circumcision

**Scapegoat**  the person who is blamed for the misfortunes of a group

**Sephardim**  Jews whose ancestors came from Mediterranean countries such as Spain, North Africa and the Middle East

**Shabbat**  Jewish holy day, also known as Sabbath

**Shalom**  Hebrew for 'peace'

**Sheloshim**  thirty days of mourning after the death of a relative

**Shema**  'hear!'; the Jewish prayer stating the oneness of God

**Shiva**  'seven'; the first seven days after the death of a relative

**Shoah**  'destruction'; another name for the Holocaust

**Shofar**  ram's horn used during synagogue services and festivals

**Siddur**  Jewish prayer-book

**Sidra**  portion of the Torah read during synagogue services

**Synagogue**  Jewish place of worship

**Tallit**  prayer robe or shawl worn by Jews during morning prayer

**Talmud**  collection of writings about Jewish laws and teachings

**Tefillin**  two leather boxes containing Biblical verses, worn for morning prayer on weekdays

**Tenakh**  Hebrew name for the Bible. It contains the Torah, Nevi'im and Ketuvim

**Theist**  a person who believes in the existence of a god

**Torah**  'instruction'; name given to the first five books of the Tenakh, or sometimes to the whole Bible, and sometimes to all rabbinic literature

**Vocation**  a calling by God for a special task or purpose

**Warden**  person in charge of organizing synagogue services

**Yad**  pointer used when reading from the Torah scrolls

**Yarhzeit**  Yiddish for annual remembrance of the death of a loved one

**Yeshiva**  college for rabbis and students of Jewish scripture and traditions

**Yom Kippur**  Day of Atonement

**Zealots**  Jewish freedom fighters from the first century CE

**Zionism**  belief in the need for a Jewish homeland based in the Middle East with Jerusalem as its capital

# Index